AMAZING BALD EAGLET

written by

Barbara Birenbaum

Soar like an eagle in all that you do
Barbara Biberbaum

A Story Within a Story© is two stories in one about the same theme, each uniquely different. They appear side-by-side on each page, to be enjoyed separately or together as one.

PEARTREE®

Published by
PEARTREE ®
PO Box 14533
Clearwater, FL 33766

Library of Congress Catalog Card Number 93-17659
Copyright © 1999

ISBN: 0935343-504 (HC)

Printed in the United States of America
10 9 8 7 6 5 4 3 2 1

Books by Barbara Birenbaum
  The Gooblins' Night
  Light After Light
  Lady Liberty's Light
  The Hidden Shadow
  The Lost Side of the Dreydl
  Candle Talk
  The Lighthouse Christmas
  The Olympic Glow

CIP Data
Birenbaum, Barbara

Amazing Bald Eaglet
     Summary: Eaglet goes through events of falling from its nest, only to be nurtured by both surrogate and foster eagle parents before taking flight as the Seminole Wind.
        p. cm
        1. Bald eagle-infancy. 2. Eggs-incubation.
3. Animals-Symbolic aspects - 4. Birds- Eagles - Identification
QL696.F32B57   1993, 1998
598.9'16-dc20   93-17659

Dedicated to my husband for his enthusiastic support.

Contents

Introduction

A Story. . .

This is a true story about an egg that survived an eighty foot fall to become a Bald Eaglet hatchling. To this has been added the eagle's own story as it sensed the new world from the shell of its existence until it broke through to freedom and eventually took flight as Seminole Wind.

Within A Story

The message of the Bald Eagle as a symbol of strength and resolve is revealed in one eaglet's trauma and survival after being displaced from its family and nest. The eagle takes wing after being nestled and nurtured by surrogate parents and tended by foster parenting eagles on its way to maturity when it soars as a messenger to man to nurture nature.

EAGLET LANDING

Eagles are known for the breadth of their wing span and the altitude of their flights. But, how many become known for the distance they fall, especially one that does so before birth as an eaglet egg, or egglet?

Since ancient times, eagles have been regarded as symbols of courage and power because of their size, keen vision, strength and the altitude to which they soar.

2

This is the story of a Bald Eaglet hatchling, a Sea Eagle or Erne. It is also known as the American Eagle, since it lives near shores of lakes, streams and coastal regions of North America.

The American Eagle can be found as far north as Alaska and Canada. It spans the continent, with nests from Florida to the east and California to the west. It can sleep wing-wide in the air, and is known for its skill and beauty of flight.

Like people of the world, eagles come in all sizes, colors and shapes. Large Golden Eagles, common in the Rocky Mountains and Pacific coastal ranges, build nests on tops of trees or ledges of cliffs usually inaccessible to man. Others of the genus, Aquila, include stately Imperial Eagles of Asia, Spotted Eagles of central and southern Europe, Dwarf Eagles of Europe, India and Africa, Sea Eagles, and Tawny Eagles.

The events that follow could have happened to any eaglet of North America.

In the fall, a pair of Bald Eagles homed a nest high in a tree near Lake Seminole, on the gulf coast of Florida. This area, near the mouth of Tampa Bay, was the nesting territory of many eagles.

Thus, this eaglet's beginning seemed as common as eggs to a nest.

These large birds of prey of the family, Accipitridae, also include kites, hawks, buzzards and vultures. They are recognized by their powerful hooked bills, well-developed legs and feet with toes that have long, curved talons. Their broad wing spans support them on long, soaring flights.

However, Seminole Wind followed its own direction in life to become an amazing bird! As winter encroached on the season, it was an eaglet egg being warmed and protected in a nest by its parenting Bald Eagles. That is, until the tree was toppled.

Though they nest in all types of trees, including dead trees, families of eagles often return to the same territory year after year to hatch their young.

While some nests are used every year, some eagles build two nests, using them on alternating years. Nests added to every year eventually topple of their own weight.

Most birds take flight *after* birth, but as the tree fell, the nest and eaglet egg took wing! Its unbroken landing on the ground had an impact on mankind and became recorded in history. No one knew whether the egg had survived the free fall flight. Until it hatched, it wouldn't know that either!

But this infringement almost cost this Bald Eaglet-Egglet its very existence!

Creatures of nature have survived the trauma of mankind's encroachment on their territory. With the development of landscaped living, eagles have been forced to relocate their nests to higher limbs, out of harm's way.

They have been known to build nests near ball fields, in subdivisions by roads and even on cellular phone towers. But, eagle nests on man-made structures are rare.

THE LUCKY EGG

It was a crisp, cool evening when the egg dropped eighty feet to the ground. There it sat for almost fifteen hours until it was discovered uncracked in the remains of the nest the next morning. It later hatched under extraordinary circumstances.

Eaglet eggs are about three inches long, short to oval and bluntly rounded on the ends. They are bluish-white and often nest stained. The inside shell is lined with membranes. The hard, outer shell is a protein skeleton with heavy deposits of calcium carbonate and other minerals. It is marvelously adapted to bear the weight of the incubating parents.

This quarter pound egg was called, "pretty lucky", amazing everyone that it didn't break upon landing. It was too soon to know whether the eaglet inside had survived. The trauma of the fall may have been felt by the egglet from the *inside*. Later, it would be sensed by the eaglet from the *outside*, as just another obstacle for one of nature's creatures to overcome in order to survive.

Eagles mate for life and build massive stick nests, or aeries, that can be up to twelve feet deep and eight feet across. They are found on the ground, rocky cliffs, or high in trees, near wetlands, coastal areas, or by large lakes and rivers. Like homes, they are repaired and added to each year.

The parenting Bald Eagles were traumatized by the displacement of their nestling. Some eagles spend an entire season rebuilding a nest, or aerie. Then, they wait until the next breeding season to mate and raise eaglets.

Had this Bald Eaglet been hatched and brooded in this nest, it would be easier for it to return to as an adult. But for now, this eaglet was a displaced Bald Eaglet-Egglet without a home.

Since eagles respond to many more sights and sounds than man, it could have used its acute sense of smell to mark an odor map of where to return to its territorial home, or nesting, when it became an adult!

Eagles have five directional information sources to locate their homing sights. They use topographical features, including the wind, the sun, the stars, and the Earth's magnetic fields, as well as odors.

10

SURROGATE PARENTING

This amazing eaglet-egglet was almost ready to hatch when found! It was rushed to a new home at the Audubon Society's Center for Birds of Prey. There, it joined another egg being nestled and nurtured by surrogate Bald Eagle parents, Prairie and T.J., each missing a wing. Within minutes, Prairie had rearranged the nesting material and returned to her incubating posture.

The size of the air sac of the egg reflected in bright light determined the prenatal age of the egg. The hatching period for Bald Eagles is between thirty-three to thirty-five days.

Some birds begin to incubate as soon as the first egg is laid. Most wait until the clutch is complete. This results in all of their eggs hatching at about the same time. Thus, the parents can devote undivided attention to their young.

In the meantime, the biological parents seemed to be recovering from the trauma of losing their eaglet egg. Only two days after the loss of their aerie, or nest, they were seen performing mating rituals, while flying over the lake. They had taken up new residence inside the wildlife preserve of Lake Seminole Park.

Eagles of displaced nests either find an abandoned one, or start a new nest, if one cannot be found. Habitat selection enhances their survival. There is a transition from courtship to nest building, brooding and parenting.

Since Florida is the home to more eagles than any other state than Alaska, there is always a chance of spotting one. Some eagles are year round residents, while others go north in the winter. Often, empty nests get destroyed or habituated by Great Horned Owls.

Had this eaglet-egglet started its life in any other area of the country, it might have been brooded by a White-tailed, Steller's or Golden Eagle, all relatives of the Bald Eagle.

Steller's Sea Eagles are similar to Bald Eagles in appearance, while White-tailed Eagles resemble the Bald Eagles, but lack white heads. White-tailed Eagles are an Old World Species, restricted to the Aleutian Islands of North America.

Golden Eagles live on mountain-sides and canyons, and open prairies and grasslands of the western states. Their winter habitat is throughout much of North America except the southeast.

Golden Eagle

White-tailed
Eagle

Like other creatures of nature, eagles have learned to adapt to the urban landscape of man. This is so essential to their survival. And this eaglet, that was still an egglet, had to adapt to a new home with a surrogate family!

Eagles live about fifty years and usually mate for life. Bald Eagles, White-tailed Eagles and Steller's Sea Eagles are similar in appearance and emit the same harsh, metallic cackling sounds.

Adult Bald Eagles range in size from 21 to 32 inches. They have about 7000 feathers. A Whistling Swan has the most with more than 25,000 feathers. In general, the smaller the bird, the more feathers it has.

Steller's Sea-Eagle

14

A BOUNCING EAGLET

Just as the egg was feeling warm and secure, Prairie showed signs of agitation - an indication that hatching time was near. The eaglet pecked at the shell and Prairie changed from the incubating posture to the more upright hatching posture. The next night it had pecked nearly three quarters of the way around the egg, hatching completely the next morning.

Like other chicks, an eaglet, gets out of its shell using an "egg tooth" and strong "hatching muscles" on the back on the head and neck. After swallowing much of the liquid in the egg when ready to hatch, it pulls the membrane-wrapped yolk into its abdomen.

It works its head into the air-space of the egg to breathe and peep. The "egg tooth" is forced against the shell, making the first hole, when the hatching muscles contract. Head and leg movements complete the breakout.

One week to a day after the nest fell to the ground, a healthy and hungry chick about three inches tall emerged. It weighed less than a quarter of a pound, wobbled unsteadily and peeped heartily, letting everyone know of its arrival! Prairie and T.J. took turns sitting on another unhatched egg and feeding the newly hatched eaglet bits of fresh fish.

Hatchlings occur more often in mornings, allowing for feedings by night.

All Eagles are fish eaters and known for thievery. Breeding pairs usually require up to 15 square miles for hunting food. White-tailed Eagles follow salmon runs, for a steady supply of dying fish.

Golden Eagles can overtake ducks in midair and chase down rabbits. The voice is generally not heard except for occasional mews or yelps.

16

When the eaglet stayed healthy and hardy beyond the critical first two days of life, it proved to itself and others that miracles do happen, even to the smallest creatures of the world.

Its dark, downy coat changed several times within the first few days after birth.

Young Bald Eagles, the second and third year birds, are called, "White-bellies," with white streaking on stomachs, under the wings and backs.

Bald Eagles are not bald, but develop white feathers on the head and neck, and tail by age three, that contrasts with the brownish-black plumage. They have no feathers on the lower legs.

White-tailed Eagles have pale brown feathers and a cream colored, stubby tail. The Steller's Sea Eagle is also white-tailed. Golden Eagles have golden highlights on the crown and nape.

As the eaglet started its new life outside the shell of its existence, it was not only cared for by the Bald Eagles in the nest, but also attracted much attention from the media and people everywhere.

As often as eagles can be spotted soaring in the sky, how often can one be watched as it is nurtured into "being"?

This was the first Bald Eagle born in captivity in Florida since the 1940's and the only bird known to survive such a traumatic fall. Since eggs are also damaged by chill, it was given a ten percent chance of survival because it cooled as it lay unprotected on the ground for so long. But, the survival rate increases the closer the egg is to gestation, or time to hatch.

Eggs cushioned within nests that become dislodged, especially large ones like eagle aeries, have a greater chance of survival.

The surrogate Bald Eagles, Prairie and T.J. were wonderful at nurturing. But with injured wings, they could not teach eaglet chicks to fly! Five weeks after hatching, this chick was resettled in a foster nest containing two other eaglets of the same size. The parenting eagles tended to it as if it was their own.

The eaglet hatchling had a caring foster family and a home!

Brooding is the protective way eagles sit on eggs until they hatch. After the eggs hatch, eagles also brood, or tend, the new hatchlings. The major parenting duties are to keep the young safe from predators and watch over them as they feed.

Both parent eagles help in rearing the young. The male gets more food, while the female does more brooding. Eaglets are taught what to eat, how to find it, and how to handle it. Because they grow so rapidly, they go through enormous amounts of food! Parenting eagles cease caring before the eaglets are ready to be on their own.

THE MESSENGER
TAKES WING

The eaglet was also called a Bald Eagle chick! These two names were more than sufficient for one of nature's endangered species. Bald Eagles no longer need the Endangered Species Act protection, however harassing them is punishable by law.

It was also given the name, Seminole Wind, after the city and lake in Florida, close to where it started its life and where it might take up territorial rights when it takes wing.

John James Audubon, the French-born American naturalist and painter, misidentified the young Bald Eagle, not realizing that even mature birds that are fully grown, don't acquire the distinctive white head and tail until their fourth or fifth year. He called it the Washington Sea Eagle.

The foster parent Bald Eagles seldom left the eaglets alone in the first few months of life. Many demands were made on them. The mother fed and brooded them, protecting them under her wings, while the father brought them food.

Bald Eagles are thought to be clumsy in hunting and fishing, eating injured or dead fish. Perhaps their acute sense of smell picked up odors from land and sea wafted on the breeze to catch their prey. How else could they hone in to steal live fish caught in the mouths of other birds, like the osprey?

Although they can fly, eaglets stay near the nest being fed prey. Slowly, the birds grow stronger as the quills, or larger wings and tail feathers, have time to harden.

Between four and twelve months after hatching, this eaglet learned to catch its own prey and make its own nest.

After three to five months, eaglets develop to adult size, grow feathers and learn to feed themselves and take their first flight. Since sex of wild birds is determined by size, it was several months before Seminole Wind was known to be a female, larger than her male counterpart.

Seminole Wind was a very amazing egg that survived the eaglet landing! Caring people and good nurturing also helped it overcome its unusual beginning. It has shared the nesting of biological, surrogate and foster parenting Bald Eagles, and holds a unique identity as a bird of prey.

The Bald Eagle was revered, sacred and honored by natives of North America. On totem poles it represents clans of Indians. Its feathers were used as both ceremonial objects and on headdresses.

The Bald Eagle was voted by Congress to be the national emblem of the new nation in 1782. That was five years before the Constitution was drafted.

The gentle, seasonal wind cradled its eighty foot fall as an eaglet-egglet. As a Bald Eagle, it is a symbol of strength and reserve.

When it soars as the Seminole Wind, it spreads its wings as a messenger to man to nurture nature and temper progress.

Thomas Jefferson praised the Eagle as, "A free spirit, high soaring and courageous." Benjamin Franklin considered it a bird of bad moral character like those among men who live by "sharping and robbing."

Audubon wrote, "If America has reason to be proud of her Washington, so has she to be proud of her great Eagle."

Every person carries the message of Seminole Wind, to be nurtured and loved, so they can soar like the eagle to meet the challenges that face them in their tomorrows.

EAGLE FLIGHT

Sight of the eagle,
soaring to heights,
symbol of freedom,
powerful bird in flight,
nurtures its passage
over fields and plains.
The proud, Bald Eagle,
over the land it reigns.

Nesting by coastal waters,
high in cliffs and trees,
it guards our country,
gliding from mounts to seas.
Broad winged eagle,
head crowned in white,
with its keen vision
maps out its flight.

Messenger of America,
emblem of the land,
free spirit, high soaring
guardian of man.

Barbara Birenbaum
Naturalist

26

For further reading

BIRDS. Barbara Taylor. (Dorling Kindersley, NY), 1995.

BIRDS OF TROPICAL AMERICA. Steven Hilty. (Chapters Publishing LTD., Shelburne, VT.), 1994.

FAMILIAR BIRDS OF SEA AND SHORE. National Audubon Society Pocket Guide (Alfred A. Knopf, NY), 1994.

FIELD GUIDE TO THE BIRDS OF NORTH AMERICA. National Geographic Society), 2nd ed., 1987.

LAND OF THE EAGLE. Robert McCracken Peck. (Summit Books, NY), 1991.

NORTH AMERICAN BIRDS OF PREY. National Audubon Society Pocket Guide. (Alfred A. Knopf, NY), 1994.

RETURN OF THE EAGLE. Greg Breining. (Falcon Press Co., Inc., Helena, MT), 1994.

THE BIRDER'S HANDBOOK. Paul R Ehrlick, David Dobkin, Daryl Wheye. (Fireside Books,NY), 1988.

THE SECRET LIVES OF BIRDS. Pierre Gingras (Firefly Books, Buffalo, NY).

Acknowledgments to the following Wildlife Artists and Photographers:

Dick Ayre: Pen and ink illustrations
            Pages iii, 1, 4-7, 11, 15-17, 21, 23-24, 26.

Rick Denomme: Photographs
            Back cover, and pages 2-3, 10, 18, 20, 25.

Sharon A. Savastio: Photographs
            Front cover, and pages 8, 12, 19.

Special thanks to the National Geographic Society for granting permission for the reproduction of Golden, White-tailed, Steller's Sea Eagles and Bald Eagles from THE FIELD GUIDE TO THE BIRDS OF NORTH AMERICA, 2nd Edition, on pages 13, 14 and 22 of this book.

Special thanks to the following publishers for granting permission for their books to be referenced *For Further Reading* : Alfred A Knopf, Chapters Publishing LTD., Dorling Kindersley, Falcon Press, Firefly Books, Fireside Books, The National Geographic Society, and Summit Books.

DICK AYRE: Wildlife Artist

Dick catches life in the eyes of animals and conveys the character of each in pen, ink and brush art. This has earned him awards in judged and juried shows throughout Florida. His wildlife drawings have been published in the Florida Audubon Society's, *Naturalist Magazine*, and the Audubon book, THE YOUNG NATURALISTS. The Conservation Association has selected pieces to promote Florida's natural wildlife preservation. His work can be found in many galleries and gift shops along the gulf coast of Florida.

RICK DENOMME: Wildlife photographer

Rick and his wife, Connie, of Northville, Minnesota, have been professional photographers for more than fifteen years, traveling throughout the world to capture the natural images of animals on land and sea. Each and every image has been produced in the darkroom of their home. Their wildlife photography is found throughout the midwest and south.

SHARON A. SAVASTIO: Wildlife Photographer

Sharon is an award winning wildlife and nature photographer whose photographs convey a message of conservation and concern. The viewers have the opportunity to experience an intimate moment with nature's image, forever preserved. Exhibitions include Boyd Hill and Moccasin Lake Nature Parks, Ducks Unlimited, Tampa Bay Wildlife Federation, Lowry Park Zoo and Red Cloud Gallery.

BARBARA BIRENBAUM: Author and Naturalist

You may know Barbara as an author of nature and historical events, blending fact with adventure, but probably didn't know she is an avid naturalist who was always surrounded by uncanny pets. She gives character to and personifies the animals in stories, nurturing the unique nature of their being.

The happenstances of this Bald Eagle begin when it is an eaglet-to-be, or eaglet-egglet, sensing the world from the inside out. The events that occur as the egglet hatches to become a Bald Eaglet are finely woven in a story, nestled in a more factual Story Within a Story© about Bald Eagles. To this are added pen and ink drawings and photographs. It is also about biological, surrogate and foster parenting eagles, and the impact one bird has on mankind.

Barbara is a literary representative for the State of Florida, Division of Cultural Affairs, and served two years as a poet of Pinellas County, Florida, Arts in Education. She was an author honoree at the Adler Literary Conference, the Statue of Liberty and Groundhog Day Centennials. THE OLYMPIC GLOW was in the Curriculum Guide to the Atlanta Centennial Olympic Games. Her poetry has received Awards of Excellence and been semi-finalist in Open Juried Contests. Her melodies, including *Eagle Flight* of this book, have been recipient of Special Popular Music Awards by ASCAP, The American Society of Composers, Authors and Publishers.